How to Start, Run and Grow a Successful Thrift Store Business On & Offline

How I Opened My First Store for Under $10K

Step By Step Guide

By

Julie Hoffman

Copyright (C) 2016 CSB Academy Publishing Co.

All rights reserved. In accordance with the U.S. Copyright Act of 1976, the scanning, uploading, and electronic sharing of any part of this book without the permission of the publisher is unlawful piracy and theft of the author's intellectual property. If you would like to use material from this book (other than for review purposes), prior written permission must be obtained by contacting the publisher. Thank you for your support of the author's rights.

CSB Academy Publishing Company

P. O. Box 966

Semmes, Alabama 36575, USA

Cover Design

by

David Miller

First Edition

TABLE OF CONTENTS

1. What is a Thrift Shop?...5
2. Why It Is a Good Investment 9
3. How Much Money Does It Take?.......................................16
4. What are the Requirements for Opening a Thrift Store? ...20
5. 5 Steps to Open Your Own Thrift Store Business 25
    1. Legal Entity Information 25
    2. Picking the Right Location 28
    3. Design Your Store's Layout 29
    4. Setting up the Store...30
    5. Decorating Your Store 30
6. 5 Ways to Get Inventory for Your Store 31
    1. Online Wholesalers and Retailers....................................31
    2. Faith-Based Community Centers and Churches 31
    3. Garage Sales...33
    4. Goodwill and Salvation Army Stores During Sales..........34
    5. Local Classified Ads 34
7. How to Price the Merchandise 36
8. 6 Great Ways to Market and Promote Your New Store 41
    1. Your Online Presence..42

2. Your Employees Are Your Best Marketing Asset.............42

3. Via Online Marketing Ads 43

4. Word of Mouth 45

5. Weekly Sales 46

6. Offering Discounts to Special Groups of People.............46

9. 4 Tips to Maximize Profit and Become Successful 47

1. Buy Off Season, Sell On Season 47

2. Be Picky About What You Buy for Your Inventory 47

3. Knowledge is Power, So Know Your Products Before You Buy 48

4. Price Right 48

10. How to Maximize Profit...50

11. The Last Word 54

1. WHAT IS A THRIFT SHOP?

A thrift shop is a store that sells different types of second-hand merchandise like clothes and household items in the pursuance of raising money for charity. Thrift stores are different from resale or consignment stores. They are typically run by non-profit organizations instead of profit driven individuals and gravitate towards a mission that most of the time invokes the greater good. Some of the best examples of thrift stores in the USA are the Goodwill shops and Salvation Army. These thrift stores can be found throughout the United States, mainly in cities, and reach spectacular numbers such as 1600 Salvation Army stores and more than 2600 Goodwill stores.

Since a thrift store gets its merchandise mainly from donations or by paying a small percentage of the actual selling price for every item, it allows them to make money even if their product prices are very low. Also, the merchandise in thrift stores varies and is frequently changing. This means that you will be able to find something new every time you visit a thrift shop. Because of this, some people like to go to thrift stores not because they have financial problems or because they want to buy the same products they will get at a regular shop for a fraction of the price, but because they actually enjoy the thrill of the chase and the novelty that you can get only from a thrift store.

A typical thrift store is usually divided into sections, according to the types of merchandise they sell. For example, most of them have a large clothing section where you can find casual wear, children's clothes, and even business wear But depending on the thrift shop you find, it could also sell household items, toys, appliances, furniture and even books. In fact, there is no limit on what you can find in a thrift store. Unlike a regular shop, where you find products that are demanded with regularity, in a thrift store you can also find the most obscure objects like collectibles, rare items, and memorabilia.

All the items in a thrift store are reduced to a third, or even lower price compared to what you might find in a retail store for the exact same item. These are what makes the thrift store so appealing... the unlimited possibilities and variety. Couple these with the specially lowered prices, and you have a great alternative to a regular retail store, as long as you are not too picky and can bear in mind that you are not the first person who has used that product or wore those clothes.

A thrift store is a great place to buy stuff at a fraction of the retail price and discover things you never knew existed. But if you don't get your expectations straight you may be a bit disappointed. You see, a thrift store is not built to be a high-end retail but rather a more decent platform for second-hand product exchange. Because most of the products are either donated or purchased at a very low price, you must not set your expectations too high when it comes to the quality of the products.

As I said earlier, the products are second hand and their usage varies from item to item. Because of this you should expect to find items from all categories of usage, ranging from new and almost new to severely used. Many thrift stores do not even have changing rooms, so keep that in mind… in most cases, you cannot try on the clothes you buy.

Another downside of thrift stores is the lack of certain clothing sizes. This happens because most of the clothes are donated and are representative of the people who donated them. Knowing all of the above, you are now able to have a broad comprehension about the thrift stores near you. Whatever the case may be, know that most of the money you spend in a thrift store goes either to a church or some charity, sometimes schools or rehabilitation programs.

This means that with every purchase you are helping to reduce waste and at the same time help your community. For example, the Goodwill thrift stores help different programs like workforce placement and job training that helps integrate minorities into the job market. In other words, shopping at the thrift store is a superb way in which you can save money and also contribute to the development of your community.

I have only mentioned the cases in which the thrift stores are used as a means of generating funds for churches, NGO's and other humanitarian purposes, but the thrift store can also be a profitable business, deployed in the pursuance of generating profit for personal causes. In the next chapter I will explain why the thrift store business model is a good investment.

2. WHY IT IS A GOOD INVESTMENT

There is a popular American saying that everyone has to step in a thrift store at least once in their lifetimes to experience the real freedom of exploration and infinite possibilities. I don't know if this is the best way to experience the ultimate freedom of exploration, but I do know that a very large percent of the American population regularly shops at thrift stores to save money or simply because it is a cool way to find new conversation starters that you can decorate yourself or your space with.

Some people find it very difficult and costly to purchase the living essentials when they change homes or when they move on their own. It might not seem like much, but the combined purchasing of everyday items such as cutlery, mugs, home decorations and every little thing you need when you move into a new space can reach astronomical scores. So why not purchase these kinds of everyday items in bulk from your local thrift store at a fraction of the original cost? Why not indeed.

This is why so many youths choose to first supply themselves from a thrift store with what necessities they can find, and only then go purchase the rest from everyday retail shops. This way they manage to save a great amount of money and invest it in something else. So do older people when they want to buy stuff, but lack either the time or the finances to go to regular retail shops.

Besides these two categories, there are also the pickers and collectors that regularly browse the local thrift stores in search of old items that might also have a monetary value.

I personally know a lot of people who do not lack the money needed to shop from everyday, regular stores but prefer the thrift store because they feel for their communities or actually like to save money. This is why, as a thrift store owner, you will not lack the needed customers to make your business profit. In the current state of the economy, and because people are starting to learn more sustainable ways of living, thrift stores are becoming more and more prevalent throughout the world, and the United States is no exception.

Many people shy away from opening their own thrift store because they either do not see the value of it, they don't believe they can make enough out of it, or they simply do not know where to get the merchandise to sell. In the pages to come, I will explain how you can get high-quality merchandise for a newly opened store and how actually to make your thrift store profitable. Just bear with me.

I'll start by saying that people are actually used to donating the belongings they have no need for any more. Clothes that do not fit them anymore, kitchen utensils that have been replaced with other more efficient ones, toys that have no use anymore, and sporting equipment or electrical devices. These are all parts of a list of objects that people donate because they do not need them anymore, and because by doing so they find a sense of contributing to the community.

Many people that donate their clothes and other goods to thrift stores for charity do not even know that only a small percent of the profit goes to the charity that it is intended for. The rest is used for salaries and reinvestment. In some cases, when the thrift is not run by an NGO, the donated items are even sold for a profit. The amount of profit that some of the thrift stores in the US make is outrageous to say the least. This is because they have legal expenses with the acquisition, and they only need to pay the rent for the location where the business operates, the salaries and the utilities. The rest is pure profit.

I learned from someone who helped open thrift stores around the country that the biggest impediment all thrift stores face in their early days is with their acquisition of materials. As you might have expected, acquiring quality merchandise can be a bit troublesome at first. Some seek help from a charity that they affiliate with. The name and notoriety of that charity is, in some cases, enough to bring people together and generate enough donations to get a head start. But the actual affiliation with a charity involves extra cumbersome legal steps that scare people away.

Another way to get quality merchandise is to advertise online. I find that setting ads online that promise a couple of bucks for a pound of clothes usually does the trick. Just remember to get there and collect your clothes for yourself. And of course also remember to include that in your advertisement.

No one wants to travel around with a pound of clothes in a busy city, so you must be able to go and pick up the donations or purchased second-hand materials yourself. Remember also to list your phone number or another way for donors to get in contact with you and you'll be off to a great start.

Some experts say that it is much more efficient to go and collect the second-hand merchandise for yourself than to wait for people to come to your shop. Another great strategy you can use when buying certain categories of products is to ask for donations. People usually love to donate, since they feel like they are doing a good deed. So when you go to buy clothes, furniture or footwear from someone, ask if they have anything else they would like to donate. This usually works and you end up with other free materials you can sell in your thrift store.

Starting a thrift store requires some amount of capital that can vary widely depending on scale, store location, and other logistical aspects. Depending on your initial business plan, you can choose from the two options that I have mentioned earlier: the one that involves the implication of a non-profit organization or the one in which you are on your own. You must choose carefully and take every aspect into consideration when you make this choice, since it has a high probability that it will forever influence the further development of your business.

Now let's talk about the thrift store being a good financial investment. A thrift store can be as profitable as its management allows it to be. Of course, there are other aspects you must take into consideration when attempting to open your own thrift store business. Some of the other things you must take into consideration are the size you want your store to be and the type of products you will offer to your clients. Some thrift stores specialize in furniture, clothes or other products according to local demand.

According to the National Association of Resale Professionals, the Goodwill thrift shop chain generated about $3 billion annually in retail sales. That is huge! But also take into consideration that they are the biggest thrift shop enterprise in the US, with a bit over 2,500 stores nationwide.

So, until you reach those astronomical scores, you will have to deal with smaller sums of money and a lot of work that needs to be done. Two more examples of fortune generation thrift stores are The Buffalo Exchange with $70 million in yearly revenue and California's Crossroads Trading which generated an average of $740,000 per store. I put these numbers here not to discourage you or create false hope, but to show that the thrift store business is booming and, contrary to public belief, serious money can be made out of it.

But don't calculate your profits before you reach home. Thrift stores, like any other business, have a lot of expenses that come with the package. In order to calculate the net income, we must subtract the overheads and cost of sales from the revenue.

The usual expenses generated by a regular thrift store include utilities, rental, staff salaries, communications and other taxes. All of this and much more must be taken into consideration when wanting to open a brand new store. Neglect enough variables and you will find yourself in a critical situation in no time at all. This is why, before you start, you must devise a very elaborate business plan. There are thousands of good models online that can help you build your perfect business plan, and once you do you can also use it to get loans or help from specialized individuals like business angels.

The Buffalo Exchange has more than 700 nationwide employees. If we calculate the average salary the non-supervisory staff in general merchandise stores earns, that being about $11 per hour according to the Bureau of Labor Statistics and the employees work 35 hours every week, then the total payroll of the company when it comes to employees is around $14 million per year.

Of course, your store won't be able to pay that much. But seeing these statistics will give you the algorithms needed to calculate your own sums of money. Don't forget to take all the expenses into consideration. As I said earlier, this could be extremely important and in some cases even a deal breaker.

Another cost may include purchasing the merchandise you acquire by other means than donations and auxiliary costs like heating in the winter and cooling in the summer. The average net profit margin for the furniture industry is 4.58%, and the clothing industry is 7.98%. Since these two industries are the most representative for the thrift store industry, you should expect your margin of profit to be somewhere in between.

3. HOW MUCH MONEY DOES IT TAKE?

To do this properly, you will need a pick-up truck, van or another large vehicle capable of carrying large amounts of merchandise. Remember that you will buy hundreds of pounds of clothes every day. There are the clothes and other miscellaneous items that you can't put into your thrift store either because you don't carry such items or because they might be in such bad shape. Whatever the case, if you want to make a profit fast, don't turn down any donations. Think about selling them to rag shops and other similar businesses or even recycling. You can often purchase and/or sell stuff either by item or by the pound.

I opened my very first thrift store for little under $10,000. This is how I did it.

I already had a truck, so I didn't pay anything for a vehicle. My suggestion is not to buy a truck or van at first, but make do with what you have and if you need a big vehicle for specific items you can just ask a friend for help.

I spent a total of $300 for licensing, filing the LLC, EIN, etc.

I rented a 2900 square-foot storefront for $1800 a month and paid the first month's rent with two months free when I agreed to a three-year lease.

I then paid $1550 to fix up the store since it needed some VCT (commercial vinyl floor tiles) tile replaced, a fresh coat of paint and the bathroom needed a new sink and toilet. Then I had to add some lighting.

Next, I found most of my store fixtures and clothing racks (even a checkout counter) from a store that was closing down in our area. I paid $1750 to buy them.

Then I bought a cash register from Amazon for $375.

Lastly, I bought my entire inventory from shoes to books to clothing (mostly clothing) and even some furniture, toys, and accessories for $3400.

Three days before we opened I paid $500 for various promotions, ads for the grand opening and yard signs.

The grand total for this store's opening cost came to $9675, still under $10,000.

The cost of opening a thrift store varies according to what you already have. For the purpose of trying to make an estimate for you, I will not include the cost of purchasing your actual merchandise. The reasons for this are that the actual merchandise cost is very little, and most of it is donated anyway.

What really matters are the other expenses. Apart from the previously mentioned vehicle, which you probably already own if you are thinking about starting this type of business, there are also some legal expenses you must take into consideration such as getting a license. Setting up your store with everything it needs (including fitting rooms, if you want to gain an edge over your competitors) can cost quite a bit, but it's important to decorate everything nicely and create an environment that will actually make people want to shop there.

Racks, Hangers, even mannequins are extremely pricey, but don't worry, since second-hand items will become your area of expertise. Here's a pro tip: get them at the big stores that don't use them anymore. They literally throw away hundreds of hangers, so maybe they'll be happy to donate a few. Look for such items that you can use in your store outside retail shops where they usually throw their stuff away, and I promise you will find small treasures.

With these expenses covered including rent, opening up a thrift store will cost you somewhere between five and ten thousand USD. However, no one can give you an exact estimate because it depends immensely on the resources that you already have or that you can get for little or no cost at all.

A cash register and expenses, with advertising, are also not to be dismissed so easily. Luckily, we live in the era of the Internet. Online advertising and social media platforms are not only some of the most effective ways to advertise because they reach a large number of people in a very short time, but don't require much effort to find a bargain. Most of the time you are sure to find a bargain.

4. WHAT ARE THE REQUIREMENTS FOR OPENING A THRIFT STORE?

First of all, let's get the boring stuff out of the way. In order to open a thrift store or any kind of business, you will have to register it and get a license. The process and cost of getting this kind of license and registration may vary from state to state or according to what your business intends... namely charity or profit. However, in most states, this license is called a reseller license or sales privilege license.

Second, consider what payment methods you will make available in your store. Accepting only cash and checks means you need no more than a simple cash register. We already included the cost of a cash register in the previous chapter, but consider this: these payment methods are not enough if you want to get a really big profit. If you want to do that, you will also need to accept credit cards. But in order to do that; you'll also have to increase your starting cost.

You will need to create an account with a firm that oversees these electronic transactions. It is really up to you to decide what you will do. Opening with just cash spares you a lot of money when you are just beginning, but it's a slippery slope in the sense that you might lose clients that wants to use their card when shopping.

There are certain methods which can help you and your store with accepting credit cards. By choosing the smarter methods, you can greatly reduce the costs associated with that. Merchant accounts imply that you will need a person or usually a company that manages these transactions for you and makes sure the money you receive from your customer ends up in your bank account. If you are also selling online, it's a bit different as well. The best way to ensure that you are covered on all fronts when it comes to offering multiple payment options is to have a POS system. Sure, it can be costly, but it is worth the investment.

Next, let's talk about the location of your thrift store. You can spare yourself the rent expenses if you open it on your own property or somewhere like a church, but if you want to make a profit in no time at all the right location is everything. It should be in an area that is easily accessible, regardless of the method of transportation. A space in an area with heavy pedestrian traffic would be perfect, but remember, it also has to be accessible by car and preferably offers the customers some parking spots.

The thrift store should be visible and look attractive to clients. There are two ways that you can play this: you can choose to be the only thrift store in your area, or you can look to lease space in an area that already has thrift stores, outlets and/or other similar stores. Each way has advantages and disadvantages.

For example, if you are opening the only thrift store in a certain neighborhood, you will be the only one to benefit from a large number of clients, but the disadvantage would be that there are a limited number of people that will come. Others will prefer stores closer to them. An opposite of that situation happens when your business is set up in an area that is especially dedicated to thrifts since people from all over will come here to look for the best bargains.

Thrift stores have increased in numbers and profits since the recession of 2008. Resale stores have always been a significant part of the American economy. According to the United States Census Bureau, its industry snapshots have shown a 39% increase in sales and 10% increase in the number of new establishments in the US. The industry has made almost thirteen billion each year according to the National Association of Resale Professionals. All the information stated above is important in regard to the potential market in which you want to open. The revenue and the business itself is a long-term investment of capital.

In order to maintain a steady flow of profit, you must first get insurance. Insurance will reduce any kind of risk exposure and will safeguard some of the most delicate merchandise inside your shop. Investing in any liability insurance is a great way of avoiding any foreseeable risks that might appear.

For example, your thrift store is selling or buying items that are inherently risky like cars or jewels. The higher price of each of these items can add up to some extra coverage or even cover legal costs in case the merchandise is stolen. Furthermore, legal costs may consist of court costs, settlements, and attorney's fees and so on; an insurance plan will cover all of this and even more to help reduce costs and protect the property of your shop.

Let's take a look at various types of insurances that you can buy in order to protect your thrift store. General liability insurance will cover any damage made to the property or injured employees. Upon buying this type of insurance, your business will be covered against disasters, employee lawsuits, and other events that might happen inside and outside of the office premises.

Business Owner Policy is another type of insurance that guarantees the value of your merchandise and equipment when lost in a fire or a lawsuit. In some cases, the damaged assets will be replaced. If the damage is done by a third party, the legal binding within a contract may provide legal fees and compensation.

The measures you take in order to minimize risk will help the owner maintain a constant carefree management. Some reports from various states have given information on how much money is lost to shoplifting and burglary, and these sums amount to tens of millions of dollars. Another approach to reducing jeopardy in your shop is to use digital unique price tags, security cameras in all the angles and keep private security guards at all entrances and exits. In case your car is used to supply and transfer different merchandise from place to place, it must first be registered at Commercial Auto coverage.

5. 5 STEPS TO OPEN YOUR OWN THRIFT STORE BUSINESS

1. LEGAL ENTITY INFORMATION

The first rule of opening a thrift store is to verify all the legal issues and paperwork in order to establish such a business within a state. Each state has its own legal conditions for starting a thrift store. Business taxable income or, in short UBTI, is income resulting from a trade or similar business activities carried out by this type of store; in case your profits are not related to the overall organization of profit or there is a special tax for this kind of unrelated business (non-profit).

Thrift stores can produce UBTI if the following rules apply: if the income produced from sales of goods or services, the business you are running is subject to taxation; if the type of activity carried out is the same as a commercial one, then you are subjected to taxation. Although, if you want to set up a non-profit thrift store, then the profits will go to the organization's mission to be used to support it.

UBTI does not tax income if the goods have been donated, but the goods can be sold without the generated profit to be subjected to taxation by UBTI. Furthermore, if you acquired items alongside some donated merchandise, then the purchased items are tracked differently from the donated goods and will be taxed. Another tax-exempt example is volunteers that offer a helping hand in order to run the thrift store.

The hours of work volunteers can put in are limited to each state's legislation. Some states do not provide tax exemptions for non-profit organizations. In some states, individual thrift stores that are registered as non-profit organizations must remit sales tax when the store resells or sells personal property. Depending on the profit of the store, the state may include several exemptions or not. For example, in Georgia, a thrift store that produces $500 per year is exempt from various legal taxations, while in Minnesota the exemption of tax is at a much higher yearly profit rate.

In order to set up a thrift store, clarification is needed about the type of second-hand shop it will be. There are four types of stores: pawn, classifieds, consignment and thrift. Similarities and differences between the types are subject to the way the store operates.

A consignment shop provides the customer with a place to display and sell their goods. After the merchandise has been sold, the profit is split between the customer and owner. If the goods do not sell, the customer can retrieve the items from the shop.

Classifieds stores provide a specific kind of good for sale or resale.

A pawn shop offers loans in exchange for the value of personal property or its equivalent. When the loan is repaid in the time frame agreed upon, the collateral may be then purchased back at its initial price or plus interest. In case the loan cannot be repaid, the collateral is then sold off to a pawnbroker or similar dealers.

A thrift store is a second-hand store that operates on donations but do not always work as a non-profit organization.

When someone donates or picks up goods at your store, a tax-deductible system will help you evaluate your items in order to price them correctly. Again there are advantages and disadvantages to consider. The goods are sometimes priced well under their original value, making the profit non-existent.

The catch is to either get a lot of high value items, such as cars or other high priced merchandise or get lower priced goods in great and often enormous amounts. The legal structure of the thrift store you established determines what taxes you pay. Moreover, becoming the personal accountability and governing arm of the thrift store will make you the sole proprietor of its assets and liabilities.

Additional options may include partnering up with a friend, which will bind your partnership in an agreement. Both parties must be assigned roles within the business.

Furthermore, the LLC (Limited Liability Cooperation) structure is organized under state laws and limits the personal liability of business owners. This can provide some tax advantages. For example, almost all the paperwork is done at a local IRS building. The thrift store must be included in one of the following two categories: for-profit or non-profit organization.

After evaluation, the store will be included within a category that may or may not provide the donors with tax deductions for their charitable work. Additionally, registration is required at your local business registration state office. The legal creation of the thrift store will depend on filing an Internal Revenue Service Employer Identification number, or EIN for short. The local registration will provide you with business licensing, permits and local tax registration. Some states request that you fill out a yearly report declaring the revenues produced. After all of this is done, all that remains for you to do is find a place and set up shop.

2. PICKING THE RIGHT LOCATION

The most important thing to get right from the start is the location of the thrift store. For more details check previous chapters. You will need a budget, a clear length of space in which to operate the store and all the paperwork needed to open up shop. The second step is to have a clear idea about the profile of people buying from you. The locals might prefer antiquities or European merchandise over American and so on.

Competition may make or break the future of your store, therefore it is recommended to check it out before you start your business. The third step is to determine how to sell your own brand of goods. Lots of promotional offers and discounts will be highly effective in combination with clear knowledge of what the locals look and wish for. Reward loyal customers with membership prices and offers.

3. DESIGN YOUR STORE'S LAYOUT

This is where you would also have to carefully design your store's layout and plan what product categories you will be carrying. Typically, most thrift stores carry categories like: men's clothing, women's clothing, baby clothing, toys, shoes, accessories, furniture, household electronics and equipment, books and CDs.

If you have access to a big size storefront for a very reasonable price, you may want to consider carrying some furniture along with all the other categories mentioned above. A typical thrift store is usually around 2500-5000 square feet in size, so if you can find something in between for a decent price, go for it.

4. SETTING UP THE STORE

The first things you will need when setting up your store are the fixtures and racks. Regardless of if you buy these new or used, you will be spending a lot of money. The goal is to find store fixtures that you can buy for pennies on the dollar. The best way to do this is to find a local store that is closing. They will typically sell their racks and fixtures at a greatly discounted price. There are also some used store fixture stores in every city, so do a search through the local phone book or on the internet yellow book to see who the used store fixture dealers are in your area.

5. DECORATING YOUR STORE

A fresh coat of paint can sometimes go a long way. Not to mention some locally made signs clearly identifying various areas of the store, so customers know where the toy section is versus the women's clothing section. Not only are these signs helpful, but they will also make you look professional.

6. 5 WAYS TO GET INVENTORY FOR YOUR STORE

1. ONLINE WHOLESALERS AND RETAILERS

The best place to check for furniture inventory is to look on the internet for people that are donating or selling lots of goods. You can find cheap merchandise on Amazon.com, EBay, Newegg, Bestdeals, Bonanza and Alibaba.

2. FAITH-BASED COMMUNITY CENTERS AND CHURCHES

In order to attract donations, talk to the local community centers, religious communities and welfare buildings. For example, people might buy a PC that doesn't work and then throw it away. Some of its hardware can be sold off piece by piece for a good buck. If you are not sure about how much money to spend on various small items, then check the prices on the internet via search engines. It's important to take into consideration two things: the item's age and durability. Known brands produce classical designs that hold for at least two to three years. In some cases, vintage items can sell for a nice price.

Do not start buying goods that are thirty or forty years old, because some of them might require maintenance, and you don't have the experience to evaluate the items properly.

Durability is another thing to consider. All clothes, toys, and books need to be in decent condition in order to make a small profit. It's paramount to maintain a local logistical plan, what parts of town have older people with a lot of antiques and how much you will get from doing back and forth trips for restocking from them.

The best things to get are from wealthy neighborhoods. The amount of good merchandise from these areas is huge. Having good informational contacts with people that live in such places may prove a good source of income in the long term. Also, try going out of state for some goods. You never know what kind of cool stuff you could find at a low price.

Before we dig deeper into the knowledge of items and merchandise to sell, a vital fact must be first addressed: namely, the season in which you shop. When winter is coming, all summer articles like clothes, freezers, swimming pools and so on are priced very low. The same example applies to winter merchandise in the summer. A sure start off will be gardening tools, material, kids clothing, furniture and high school books.

Try cleaning some of the goods you invest in since furniture and clothes can be dirty or smell like cigars. Furniture brings a lot of profit if you take the time to clean, repaint and fix it. A broken chair or table might be sold off at a price of $10 or thrown out for free. In this case, fixing and repairing such an item might secure a resell price of $50-$60.

It's important to have a big car or van to take regular trips to the countryside or rural areas where you might be able to find some hidden treasures. Lots of good items can be found at low or even free prices inside local communities and towns. Find out where the elderly community likes to hang out and talk to them about different items and goods that they might have taking up space in their house. Check various Goodwill Foundations for future donations.

3. GARAGE SALES

Check out weekend garage sales in your local neighborhood. Many people like to organize garage sales on Sundays after church. Friends, relatives, and kids gather to help each other sell some of their merchandise. It can also be a good idea to visit the site of major garage sales the day after since some will leave items that didn't sell on the curb for free.

An expensive way of gathering lots of goods and merchandise will be a billboard campaign that solicits messages of donations from nearby highways, crowded areas and commuting hubs. Some billboard messages should suggest that thrift stores help you with hoarding problems or getting rid of excess items. Each donation represents a bargain, for each item donated a discount is offered or may include the possibility of donating it for a better one from the store.

4. GOODWILL AND SALVATION ARMY STORES DURING SALES

All Goodwill and Salvation Army stores have sales on various days and specific products. Call ahead to find what items are on sale on which days so you can plan your shopping accordingly. You should also learn the prime times to shop at these stores. Often when the yard sales are in full swing during the summer, there will be an increase in the merchandise available at these stores. Another good time for increased merchandise is around the holiday seasons. It is also a good idea to go earlier in the morning when there are fewer people, and you get the first choice of the merchandise.

5. LOCAL CLASSIFIED ADS

It is a good idea to run an ad on a local classified such as Craigslist, Shopper's Guide, Penny Savers, etc. Mention what types of products you are interested in buying and let the people bring the products to you so you can pick and choose what you want to buy. You can often set a price for how much you will pay for them. It is a good idea to put out these ads about four to five weeks before you open your store. The ad should read something like: "Wanted Used Clothing - Will come to your home and pick up. We pay $.12-15 a pound - Cash paid."

You can also add that you will pay higher if the merchandise is brought to you. Typically three pieces of clothing will average about a pound, so if you buy 1,000 pounds, it will translate into 3,000 pieces of clothing that will cost your around $120-$150 depending on the quality of the merchandise.

7. HOW TO PRICE THE MERCHANDISE

Pricing the merchandise in your inventory is no small task. You must first research a large range of prices in order to find the best price for your specific items. The pricing of the item must take into consideration the item's age, durability, and brand. Thrift stores have huge success because they sell good quality items at a very low price. Your merchandise should not stay in stock more than a year or two.

Famous thrift stores buy used clothes from famous brands or known brands that are in good to great condition and are about one to two years old. An average t-shirt should sell for $5 to $25 in your store. The prices must be based on factors mentioned above, and the store owner should consider raising the prices on cool shirts and sweaters to $25. People buy famous brands like Converse, Nike, Adidas and American Apparel; they sell for $10 to $25.

The magic is in the offers; you get to sell four goods at the price of three. People will enjoy spending more and more money on offers than on the items themselves. Jeans and coats go for $10, $20 or $30. Dresses go for about the same price as coats. Big stores offer various discounts, but these are few and far between. People will always sell or donate their older goods and clothes for something new in return. It's important that your inventory and stock reflect what people want to wear that season. Individual wardrobes are constantly changing or improving based on budget and bodies.

The image of a thrift store is very important and changing your exhibits monthly will guarantee that people will remain interested in your merchandise. Holidays and seasons only last for a couple of days or weeks at most. Promotional goods have a short shelf life during these times if you are going to have a profitable store. Adding messages that announce new stocks of merchandise and stock clearances will entice people into visiting your shop frequently.

The items left on shelves or in warehouses must be paired/grouped with new items or with bundles. If you order new goods to place on display, make sure you have some less appealing items nearby in the reduced prices section or on offer. Pair mugs with candles, furniture with pillows and so on. Bundling them up will ensure a short sale period and clearance of all older items that don't sell easily. Choose to match the merchandise to the customer's needs. In time you will learn what loyal customers visit your shop for.

A customer always responds to things they want. For example, don't display the cheap furniture when the fancy portable kitchen table is what everyday Joe or Mary wants. Just because they need a new, cheap table doesn't mean they won't indulge themselves to the expensive model you exhibit well. Add various commercial written ads, like buy two get one free.

Each sign must be short and appealing to anyone who is interested in buying something.

In order to attract people, start putting on exhibit goods that are the closest to the front door and put your modern and most classy items in the center for attention. Be sure to have several stages of height in which to promote products, from bottom to top. Enough products must be highlighted so that the customer can pick up and touch them without having to totally dismantle your display.

Let's get to the serious part of the pricing stage. Outside factors will play a role in this phase, such as your location and the reputation of the business you own, because it must be well established. A promotional ad must be shown daily in order to paint a realistic portrait of what your clientele desires. In order to anticipate their needs and build upon a strong image, you must first create a credible marketing campaign accordingly. Never go high end with the prices, start off low and full of offers. People will be enticed to check them out. The mentality behind it is the wow factor... people will take their time and check every offer on display. Adding daily discounts on new items will sell the product quite fast.

Anyone new to this kind of bazaar will determine the price as a bargain and will buy it instantly. Each retailer will offer some kind of bundle to their offer, but instead of copying their mechanics; try a simple and familiar approach. Check out the competition's prices, inventories, and offers, make sure you know when they have discounts and bundles. Therefore, planning carefully what days you wish to start your own promotions.

Verify with online shops what new brands and items are hot sales in the particular season. Start your own website in order to promote various discounts and price reductions. Online media is a perfect place to compare products and prices so that the customer will be more inclined to this behavior. It is important to price your merchandise on what you can find on the web, take the time needed to research those goods. Once you know what prices your goods are selling for in real life and on the internet. Check your competition again and pick a day in which to discount or promote some of the bundles you have in stock.

At first, you cannot compete with big shops or huge retailers. The key here is to offer a familiar and reasonable approach to shopping. Client service must be top notch in order to achieve client satisfaction, a reference system in which clients share information about their recently purchased goods. Friends of customers will see at what prices they bought them in your store and will check out your store. When calculating prices, you need to control what you can provide at reasonable low to high price segments. Many local customers improve the overall image of your store just by recommending it to friends.

As mentioned in previous chapters, loyal customers must be rewarded in order to create a strong bond of trust between clients and store owners. Various strategies of pricing will ensure long term profits and make selling in mass an easy task. Being nice to everyone that steps inside the thrift store is equally important to the prices. To conclude, pricing is done via a lot of research of online retailers, online distributors, competition and local neighborhood shops. The price must be good and paired with lower quality items in order to secure a safe sale of all goods.

8. 6 GREAT WAYS TO MARKET AND PROMOTE YOUR NEW STORE

First and foremost you have to understand that you will be competing with names like Goodwill and Salvation Army. Sound discouraging? It shouldn't. The simple way to make yourself stand out is by the type of products that you carry in your store. Remember both Salvation Army and Goodwill operate on products that are typically donated to them.

However, your business model is different, as we discussed in an earlier chapter, "How to Get Your Inventory." Your business model is very different than theirs. Your business is not relying on donations. So you need to make that your strength and not a weakness. Since you are paying for your inventory, as I mentioned before, be very picky and buy only what is actually valuable and sellable and not junk that can just fill up your empty shelves. Try to carry many designer brands and you can even make a section in your store that shows off your best designer brands inventory.

People go to thrift stores in order to buy merchandise at a very low price. In some cases, a customer might get something incredibly good at a good price. As a new business owner with a thrift store, it can be hard to meet some selling objectives. Frustration creeps in when sales are down or when you're just not getting enough clients in your store. There are a few steps you need to follow in order to achieve a good marketing plan for your goods. These steps will teach you the basics of marketing. Let's now talk about the six proven ways you can market your store and boost sales in just 60 days.

1. YOUR ONLINE PRESENCE

People need to have a reason or motive behind their short journey to your store. One way of bringing people closer to your store is through events, limited to obtainable items exclusive to your store or website. It is imperative that you have a website in which to promote and sell your goods online. Offering online coupons will attract the attention of a lot of people. Sites like Craigslist and other famous places can be a sure and secure way of promoting your business. Another fact that needs to be weighed is in how you sell almost all of your items, merchandise, and goods that can be found in other stores and shops. People will remember their experience in your shop and therefore should always leave with a remarkable opinion about it.

2. YOUR EMPLOYEES ARE YOUR BEST MARKETING ASSET

A cost-effective way of promoting your business is through e-commercials and fundraising events within the local community. Always research what is cool and popular. When hiring new employees consider getting people who are very social, smart and well mannered. Additionally, for a customer that is always looking but never sure on buying, having employees with great communication skills will help drive sales up for your store. All of these steps make you relevant within the local community. Since your business is based on selling and reselling, communication between the clerk and customer is essential for creating a positive image about your services.

3. VIA ONLINE MARKETING ADS

This set up is perfect for the next marketing step... online bloggers. They will ruin or raise your business; they are always on the hunt for new and exciting things to promote or hinder. You can start off by paying someone to write good reviews about the merchandise on sale or offer. But the best marketing solution is the one done by a satisfied client. Good reviews and recommendations spread fast with today's technology.

Typically sponsored links or suggest links are the future of online marketing. Banner ads and product mentions are tried and true. Although they are still relevant, their cost is still high. To be perfectly clear, this type of promotion (banner ads and product mention) has less of an impact on clients nowadays. The new generation of merchandise sellers and others, like thrift store owners, have to know which site to be promoted on in order to have their business presented to the larger public online. Understanding this will help sell and reduce costs on marketing and promotional materials.

If you open up shop online or just downtown, large e-commerce websites would help you sell products online. They bring more profit in the long term, while in your spare time at home you can focus on inventory management and other chores. There have never been a greater number of places to promote or even sell your products online. Some online platforms work well together with your main website, some have replaced the need for an e-commerce website completely and work as a standalone solution for Internet-based sales and promotion.

Google can actively bring the product promotion you wish. Their software can list your business on their shopping results. This can be a great way of gaining notoriety over your local competition. Also, more online traffic on your website means more customers in the store, and that means you can easily and quickly promote various events and discounts.

If you don't have the money needed to open a thrift store, there is still hope on the Internet. EBay is a perfect platform for selling the merchandise in your inventory. EBay offers a virtual web store, meaning that alongside your business you will have a huge online retailer behind you to promote your deals. It costs a reasonable amount to have your website connected to the EBay store, but it is worth it on the long road to building your business.

Now to the print media, because, let's say you don't have the knowledge needed to improve your business on the Internet. There are still local shops, newspapers, and events where you can promote your small thrift store. This product strategy can catch the attention of the elderly community that is out of touch with the present technology.

Customers will be delighted to see your store participating in charity and welfare events. When promoting through the print media, it will cost you a hefty penny but it will be effective and should be used in seasons where other big businesses do not promote their own products.

4. WORD OF MOUTH

Word of mouth still remains a cost-effective marketing tool, it just requires a well-built promotional strategy. When customers are buying your products, encourage them to post pictures, reviews, etc. Increasing business awareness is perfect for interaction with the customers. It not only builds loyalty but it also raises the popularity of your thrift store, and the merchandise found on your shelves. This can also lead to future prospects and undiscovered goods for reselling.

5. WEEKLY SALES

Thrift stores are not only a way for people to buy pretty much anything, but they also support charitable causes and divert items from being sent to landfills. Having a weekly sale is an excellent way to boost your sales. Consider a rotating weekly sales items that have a different category every week. For example, during the holidays you can have a weekly sale themed towards that holiday. Or you can choose to have themed sales where all wood furniture is on sale or all clothing. There is no limit to the number of sales ideas you can have.

6. OFFERING DISCOUNTS TO SPECIAL GROUPS OF PEOPLE

Everyone likes to get a discount, but not every business offers a discount. Consider offering special pricing to specific groups of people such as church members, military, public service professionals, etc. Advertise these specials or have a sign in your store. These people will appreciate your deals and will be more likely to shop in your store.

9. 4 TIPS TO MAXIMIZE PROFIT AND BECOME SUCCESSFUL

1. BUY OFF SEASON, SELL ON SEASON

Think about summer clothes in the winter and in turn; your winter clothes in the summer. These are the times when people are clearing out their stores of clothing and when retail stores are putting these items on sale. Therefore, you are most likely to get your deals and the largest amount of stock in the offseason. Then you can save it and sell it during the on season for a profit. It can also give you time to make sure anything that needs cleaning or repair has enough time to get it done.

2. BE PICKY ABOUT WHAT YOU BUY FOR YOUR INVENTORY

When you are shopping for inventory, you should always keep a list. If you are going to be shopping at a store, have route planning and follow it. When you simply go into a store and wander around, you are going to be more likely to buy extra items you don't really need. At the same time, you need to keep an open and creative mind. Don't be afraid to think outside the box for items that can be re-purposed and made like new with just a little work so you can sell it for more.

3. KNOWLEDGE IS POWER, SO KNOW YOUR PRODUCTS BEFORE YOU BUY

If you have a themed store, you likely already know your items pretty well. However, if you are going to buy something, make sure you know about it first so you aren't buying something without value. For example, if you are buying furniture, be sure you know what periods and styles are popular at the time and what has the most value. This way you can be sure you are getting something that you will be able to sell in your store.

4. PRICE RIGHT

As thrift store shopping is becoming more popular, people are flocking to the stores. People go to a thrift store for a good deal, but they will also pay more for something that is nice. Therefore, it is important to know the quality and price of your products. If you price things right for a good deal, but a profit for your store you are sure to get people to buy.

Maintaining sales in the thrift store is paramount to small business success. To stay relevant in the resale market, your small store must maintain a constant flow of profit. This profit pays the company bills and leaves you enough to buy more stock items for selling. In order to do this, creative approaches will make you stand out from the competition. As mentioned previously, promotions and discounted prices on goods are vital for attracting new customers into your store. Bundle up popular items with less popular ones and you have a guaranteed sale.

Each discount encourages shoppers to spend more and more time and money inside your store. Placing valuable goods in strategic ads and shop decorations will increase the likelihood of an item being purchased by a person. Prevalent merchandise is an easy sell when offered as three at the price of two and so on.

Pricing should be around 50-75% off when you start a promotional season. Make sure you stay on top with a full stock and valuable items. Staying relevant and at odds with the competition is key when knowing promotional deals. By implementing simple strategies inside your retail store, you can increase the number of new customers just by word of mouth.

Another hefty way to increase sales is through loyalty cards to your thrift store. These cards can offer a further discount of up to 10-20% off merchandise and goods bought by customers. The cards should be given out as rewards to customers that help buy and promote your store. Furthermore, they can be used as giveaways at monthly events and seasonal promotions. Studies have shown that if you reward the customer for his loyalty and money invested in your store, he will be more tempted to continue his or her shopping sprees.

10. HOW TO MAXIMIZE PROFIT

Suggestive selling is also vital for increasing profits. For example, a customer buys a coffee cup, and your employees say, "Would you like to get the rest of the set? We have it at a discounted price." Thereby, guaranteeing a full sell of products. There are some mistakes that can be avoided when it comes to maximizing profits. New business owners should consider that profits as a goal in itself. Thrift store owners forget that a profit increase is based upon how you reinvest your capital on a short and long-term strategy.

The first step in maximizing your margins is to take into account how much money you will make on a full season and a low season. Mainly during the first two years of business, hiring an accountant is not needed. The second thing to know is how to maintain low costs in order to promote week-long sales and special prices.

Do not sell everything cheap… that can prove disastrous in the long term. Have low prices on items and merchandise you have gathered at a very low cost. Increase prices on goods such as furniture. It is a great way to make a profit. Also, reinvest some of the profit to replenish some of the goods in stock. Refurbishing is a great way to increase prices and maintain a fresh approach to how people see your goods. This might not be something new for the reader, but developing the prices and researching the market is a great way to start and to make some cash along the way.

Knowing the prices of the competition is also important in order to justify some of your own rates. Various items bring high or low numbers of profit. The dollar value of each good is appropriate to how you adjust the ratings and discounts. There are some tactics to bring more profits to the table from selling cheap items. Each paired good quality item with a low-quality item will increase its price by $2-3, which is much more than you would normally get from selling individually. Even though you might sell great amounts of goods or low amounts of quality goods, a description of the item's history and its origins should be clear and close to the product.

There are many aspects of selling inside a store or online. They all have different objectives and different budgets, but they all look for offers and discounts. Profit is linked to how well you entice a customer and how satisfied he or she is with the purchase. In the bigger picture, you have convinced a person to buy from your store more than once. A thrift store makes money just from negotiating its tariffs on the items purchased. It's important to have a good relationship with your suppliers, be involved with the process of transferring these goods in order to gain more experience in this market.

A very effective way to widen profits is to know what kind of offers attracts most people to your store. Each incentive can be

10-50% off, but that will not guarantee more customers in the store. This is why researching all the previously mentioned things will create the information needed to better plan your fiscal year and profit gain.

Note, there is no need to make drastic changes to the overall performance of your store. The store should be well organized and attractive from the moment you open up shop. The offers should be incisive and full of bundles that include good and bad merchandise. Each profit made off of the events should be reinvested in new merchandise for your stock. Again, refurbishing is a great way to increase the value of an item.

Repainting, fixing and also adding some new colors to it will increase its overall value. When you have enough money for expanding, buys lots of old furnitures and hire a few local woodworkers to refurbish them. The same goes for PC hardware. A lot of people throw out their old computers because their monitors stopped working. The pieces can be resold at a nice dollar without any risk. More details about these examples were mentioned in previous chapters.

To summarize all the facts and information about maximized profits; always remember to reinvest and research the market. All the facts and tips present must be implemented within a greater strategy of selling goods. A thrift store is a low-risk business at first, but when you grow to a middle sized retailer, the risks mount and any loss can be devastating. Small steps must be made in order to achieve a healthy profit and maintain your business through the foreseeable future. The instrument for a steady business is knowledge.

11. THE LAST WORD

If you got the idea that opening a thrift store might get you a nice profit and make for a decent living. It means that you already have a good eye for business. I won't lie to you, opening a second-hand store is no small feat. It's not easy, but I believe that with a good amount of correct information anyone can do it. A piece of final advice is to always have a vision and always set realistic goals.

Don't expect to get rich in a couple of months. Be patient and you will see your dreams come true after a normal amount of time. Also, pay a lot of attention to detail. Even the smallest detail can make or break a business.

Don't be discouraged if things are hard in the beginning. Remember to be fair to yourself and your customers. Perhaps the most important piece of advice I can give is to always pay your taxes and be accurate and precise when it comes to finances. I shouldn't have to give this advice, but there are people out there that find the paperwork and the research exhausting and might give up. Don't give up. Just go on the internet and look for recently opened thrift stores. Once you see the profit they make you will definitely regain your motivation. Most of all do it because you are passionate about it, not just for the money.

By reading this book and following all the steps in it, you should have a good starting point and a clear vision of what you need to do next. In my humble opinion, thrift stores will become more and more popular because of the situation of the economy. Besides, who says they're not fashionable? Nowadays, everybody shops at thrift stores, even celebrities.

I believe that by starting your thrift store now, it will grow fast, and you will make more than a decent living, but it all comes down to how much you are willing to work for it and how much time and money you want to invest. Nothing can be achieved without hard work, but in this case the effort you put in will be handsomely rewarded, and you will achieve your goals in no time.

Give this idea an honest try and I believe you will be successful at it.

Good luck!

www.ingramcontent.com/pod-product-compliance
Lightning Source LLC
Chambersburg PA
CBHW070408190526
45169CB00003B/1160